Rough

Cara June

Presentation by *BookLeaf Publishing*

Web: www.bookleafpub.com

E-mail: info@bookleafpub.com

ISBN: 9789360945145

First edition 2024

ACKNOWLEDGEMENT

With deep appreciation for women,
friends and lovers.

TABLE OF CONTENTS

Like Father, Like Son..1

Their Affairs..6

Limp..8

Mirror..9

How the Ruling Class Dies..13

Slattern..14

Worthless..15

Particularly American Nausea..16

Champagne Isn't Drinking..17

They (or Doris Day)..18

Serving Cunt..19

Aunts & Uncles..21

Oklahoma..22

Dworkin..24

Leaving..26

Fuck of the Century..28

Somebody Has to Die..30

Disco..31

Tori Amos..32

Lillith Fair..33

High on Fridays..35

An Ode to Bitches..36

Guilty Again..38

Italy..40

She Said..42

Desperately Seeking..44

NYE..47

Bubbles and the Oak Tree..50

Drunk Sweet..51

Hot Asphalt..54

Company Policy..58

Like Father,
Like Son

The college boys were drinking beer in the
basement,
Despite it being early morning,
Despite their being out late, and drunk, just
last night.

They decide that I'm the hottest thing
around, even if I'm close to their moms'
age.

They pretend to behave,
asking questions about my work,
while I arrange flowers to the side.
I am crouching down and moving this and
that, doing the women's work of yet another
family celebration.

I'd been running late,
so I'd quickly put my hair up in a messy bun
and thrown on a sundress in my attempt to
look festive enough and put-together.

They saw beauty and playfulness
And enjoyed my now womanly curves (tits
and ass, they say silently to each other),
scanning their young eyes over a body their
skeletal teen girlfriends would starve
themselves to avoid.

When I leave,
"I'd fuck her," he says to his friend, who
nods in agreement.

She heard him, and "no shit," she thought,
As if they know what to do with a grown
woman. She rolled her eyes.
Few men know what to do with a woman
comfortable with her body (finally),
who expects to come first.

Outside, the married men have gathered,
the fathers of the graduating girls.
Like the boys, they, too, drink beer and
survey the scene.

Tired of fucking their wives who nag them
to do their share,
Struggling to get or keep it up,
they fantasize a bit differently,

and imagine burying their faces between her
legs.

Maybe he'd come up against her,
slap that great ass,
Push her towards the table while pulling her
skirt up,
To slip his hand inside her,
from behind.

They each imagined how they could make
her come.
He believes touching her might change his
life, if he could just feel her heat,
Share her energy in a quick fuck.
For a moment, he thinks she is worth
burning his whole life down around them.

She doubts she would even get off.

Sure, they could probably have a good time.
Laugh.
Stave off the impending mid-life crisis.

When she goes to leave,
he follows.
Clumsily, he pulls her into the hallway,

trying to create a stolen moment.

She tells him that there is a difference
between a good wife and a good fuck.
"Which are you?" he asks.

For a moment, this felt more interesting than
going home,
so she poured herself another glass of wine,
adding a few ice cubes because
what difference does it make at this point,
with this crowd.
They're drinking seltzers.

She looks at him,
from a deliberate distance of a few feet
away.

"Go, be present for your good wife who has
done all of this to celebrate your daughter."

He looks at her, fighting the urge to pull her
to him.
He retreats.

She poured the rest of her drink in the sink
and went home.

He thinks about her.
It's a constant itch.

Later, while alone, he imagines tasting her.
Imagines her on top of him.
God, those magnificent tits.
Her face, beautiful but thrilling, the face of a
woman who welcomes pleasure.

He tries, but man can't get it up.
He knows she'd never fuck either of them,
father or son.
But he'll try again.

Their Affairs

Their affairs are minor indiscretions.
Forgivable.
Understandable.
Inevitable, really.

Especially the men's.
Of course, the men, with their wandering
eyes.
It's in their nature, so they've said.

Some women, too, well
with their husbands.
Their husbands are just another child to
raise.
What was she supposed to do?

But our affairs are unforgivable.
How much more do you want?
With a saint at home,
willing to love you forever,
so they say,
to women who don't uphold the deal,
the ladies who don't lunch, or play tennis
during the work day,
who never were welcome in the first place.

You can't have it all,
those women admonish us,
those who can't remember what sex can feel
like. Or maybe never knew.

Limp

Men should feel threatened by women who
love themselves
Because we stop settling for the cold.
Because it's easily replaceable.
Because we crave depth, and dimension,
and endurance,
and confidence,
and, really, you never quite had command of
the room.

Men should be threatened, greater still, by
women who love women.
The teacup on her thigh warms me more
than a man ever could.

Mirror

"We've got a plan for that,"
he says with a proud smile,
when I ask if we'll be teargassing our
students in the next few weeks.

Oh, they hope it doesn't come to that,
they tell themselves.
We just have to plan for the contingencies.
They refuse to rule it out.

These schools with their free speech centers,
institutes, explosion of new programs and
events, summits, you name it.
White man after white man coming to
campus to tell the rest of us whose speech is,
in fact, free.

Theirs is free.
Free from consequence.
Free from limitation.
Costing the rest of us plenty—
comfort
safety
dignity
our sanity

in the face of so much hypocrisy.

In fact, we pay them to tell us about free
speech.
We pay them to come insult our students and
our staff.
We call our approach "academic freedom"
but silence everyone but our oldest white
males and those who have proven that
they'll play along.

What a joke.
Sure, maybe,
Finally,
If you're faculty
(staff have no free speech rights at all)
the right kind of faculty, that is,
a good fit,
having suppressed and compromised
polished your rough edges and conquered
any rebellious spirit long ago.

How else did you get tenure?

And they play this game,
so deftly designed for the insecure.

These petty cowards aren't going to join
you, dear students.
They cross picket lines (on Zoom),
while wearing hard rock tees and talking
about protests they never attended.

By their very nature, they aren't like you.
They were desperate for the degrees you so
bravely risk. Who are they without their
PhD?

They now use their degrees to argue that
you're doing it wrong.
They support protest, of course, they say, as
they sit on their asses, comforting each other
among the fake foliage and posters with
messages promoting your well-being.

Thank you for reminding the rest of us why
we work here.
We're proud of the ways in which you are
putting yourselves into the history books,
courageously protesting genocide,
proving that there is, indeed, another way to
finance the modern university

(even if the military industrial complex
makes them the most money).
Being the last siren call against the
totalitarianism engulfing us.

They'll withhold your degrees,
per their policies,
for using what we taught you against us.

Despite all of their education,
their free speech,
their constant exploration of ideas,
their defensive posturing as champions of
dissent,
none, apparently,
knows a fascist when he looks them in the
face
in the mirror.

How the Ruling Class Dies

Pigs get fat, and hogs get slaughtered.
This is what I learned during the summer of
2002, in a miserable job in Jacksonville,
Florida.

In England, only the Queen may eat a swan,
and that about sums it up, doesn't it?
She doesn't, we're told.
Don't worry.

They're busy now eating their own, after all,
having already fleeced the rest of us.
They just forgot to hide their gluttony this
time.

Slattern

I found a new word for us.
"An untidy woman, her lipstick awry,"
per the Oxford Languages.
I love to see her smiling in the early
morning hours.

And cheers to her!
I hope the smears of her makeup are the
result of a rough and glorious night.

So take that, patriarchy.

Worthless

They're worthless.
That's all you have to say,
and we know exactly who you're talking
about.

Particularly American
Nausea

We've conquered the gag reflex.
Apparently. Otherwise,
the U.S. couldn't have made it this far.
How glorious, the ruin.
How gluttonous.
We'll eat anything they show us on Tik Tok.

As they say, there's no accounting for taste.

Champagne Isn't Drinking

I love it when the rules do not apply.
Did you know you can just decide that one
day?
To live your life the way you want to.
Have the champagne.

After all, they do.
Don't live life left out.
They'll tell you, after all,
that champagne isn't really drinking.
Have a sip.
Have a bottle.
Have another.

They (or Doris Day)

Does Kim have a sense of self?
Or is she still waiting for them to tell her?

My mother-in-law remained vigilant—
"They" said limelight hydrangeas were in
this year.
Now pickleball is all the rage.
She redecorates her homes as required by
the they-sayers.

She told me once that she used to love Doris
Day.
I swear she sat up straighter as she said it,
once she saw I was reading a book about
Elizabeth Taylor.

Someone please tell Kim you can't be Dame
Liz while desperate for approval.

Serving Cunt

I'm not sure how we ended up embracing
this as a group motto,
but it works for us.
An unapologetic rallying cry
for a group of women who resist rape
culture
It's fitting.

It's ours to serve.
Not yours to eat.
It's ours.
Ours to keep to ourselves.
To share with others.
To savor.
To stroke.
To shield.
To nurture.
To adorn.

Free.
Wild.
Ours.

They know, in all her glory,
cunt can move mountains.

Aunts & Uncles

The cool aunt has become a meme.
She drinks, she travels.
She belongs to herself.

The uncle?
At best, he's fun-loving.
An alcoholic.
The creep.

My students tell me that the "creepy uncle"
remains a thing,
so normalized
the enduring joke.

For women, the unmarried aunt is an image
of freedom.
The uncle, a sexual predator.
Interesting, isn't it?
And we laugh.

Oklahoma

I fantasized about a life in Oklahoma.
Simpler but appreciated
Full of laughter and desire

A rugged man
not afraid of me
who knew to handle me
how I wanted to be

I thought my life might be better if I lived in
Oklahoma
cause maybe there I'd feel satisfied
start a brand new life
spend more time outside
get my hands dirty
forget how it feels to cry about my perfect
lonely life

Could I leave?
I'm not going.
Not so far,
so what's holding me
here
what's holding me?

I might have never had as much fun as when
I was with Oklahoma

his fun-evil grin
right words
pulled my hair
spoke into my neck
we laughed
we fucked
we laughed again

the timing right,
will I revisit him?
will he know
how to wake me again?

Dworkin

Brutalist, radical Andrea
giving voice to our anger in legion
speaking directly without apology
so bluntly you reject her
as she describes your life to a T

She made misogyny
unforgettable
undeniable
she polished the blades so they caught our
eye,
and you hate her for it.

you want to keep hiding behind your
carefully chosen window treatments
better to decorate house than admit your
rape

she put to words the hate
men say about women
and we cast her out
she wrote about what men do
and have always done,
and we turned away

the leftist men still want bonus points
for saying sex is radical,
progressive,
liberatory,
(and it can be)
while they reenact violence from
pornography

she exposed their lies
while wearing her overalls

she shared her heartbreak with us
did we listen?
Were you bought
and distracted
in exchange for some shiny toy?

Or did you heed the call,
exact an inch,
tear by tear,
with your own sharpened blade
fighting not to stave off submission
but to reveal the full force
and might
of our full potential.

Leaving

I've got no fast car
to get me out of here.
There's no deal left to make
that will help us heal

Our sad ending.
What we've made of this marriage
loving, but hurting,
as we worked to make a living

Do I "leave tonight or live and die this way?
All at once her voice says to me
go, be free, or
stay, and be safe;
either way you have a lot to lose.
A lot.

I did leave you,
with your job that pays all of the bills
you, on your phone,
always at work
where you live

your love for me, there's no better,

you think,
you say,
but you don't know how to show

what I need is to feel an arm around my
shoulder
warm, pulling me in tight,
showing me that I belong.

I wanted us to be better.
And we got two fast cars,
that we both drive away.

Fuck of the Century

This is a story about a detective who falls
for the wrong woman.
She's the fuck of the century,
so what chance did he have?
to live happily ever after?

He called her "bitch, mostly affectionately"
He, civic-minded and respectable now,
a retired rock and roll star.

She, Hitchcock blonde
legs spread
she'd fuck for pleasure
without love
to play games
"Exactly what did you have in mind?"

He fucks another while thinking of her
Another says, "You weren't making love at
all."

You don't make love to the fuck of the
century
She likes rough edges.

She has nothing to hide.
She doesn't like to wear any underwear.
She's bemused and talks with a wink.

"Man to man, I think she's the fuck of the
century," he says.
So, you want to play hard?
Then come on.
His friend, who settled, as most men do,
replies, "Easy cowboy, I wasn't there."
Life asks them, "Are your recollections
pleasing to you?"

She and he agree:
"I'm in love with you already,
but I'll nail you anyway."
They fuck with
rough
basic
instinct.

Somebody Has to Die

Somebody has to die.
Somebody always does.

How else will we wake up?

Disco

Is any era more appealing than the heyday of
Studio 54?
How can I taste it?
Wear Halston.
Red, of course.
And dance
skate
love
fuck
feel

escape
in the beauty
and freedom
and celebration

devour the heady clouds
of glamour and ambition
longing, lust, and release
ecstasy, found in the
Last Dance.

Tori Amos

There is nothing I could write
that approaches the power of a Tori Amos
song

Have you listened to Little Earthquakes?
"These Precious Things."

Put this down right now and go listen.
Hear what it feels like to live as a woman.

Lillith Fair

I didn't go.
I was too young and too poor.
It was states away, and we just didn't know
how to do that.

But I'm glad it happened.
A brief moment celebrating "women in
rock"
As if they are few.
As if pop has no meaning.
Labeled "alternative" because they weren't
pleasant fembots.

I'm glad we got Sarah, Sheryl, Tori, Joan,
Suzanne, Bonnie, Jewel, Lisa, Natalie,
Emmylou, Fiona, Tracy, Lauryn, Mary, and
Shawn.
Amy and Emily, Liz, Meredith,
Sinéad, Des'ree, Luscious, Erykah, and the
Queen.
Women, still, on second and village stages.
Women everywhere. Safe and celebrated.

Women back-to-back won't sell, rock said.
Women are to be as few as tomatoes in a
salad, says country.
Women are to be sex objects, capitalism
said,
per the 1996 Telecommunications Act.
And we ate Britney alive.

High on Fridays

It was such relief
To get high on Fridays.

She was upset with me most other times.
An overthinker not yet over overthinking.
Still so self-conscious,
ascribing meaning to my every sigh,
to any forgetfulness (which was really due
to stress, work, age… she'll see).

But not with me.
Friday comes but once a week.
Her insecurity with that self-consciousness
ate us alive.

Discontent is her state of being,
Except on Fridays.

An Ode to Bitches

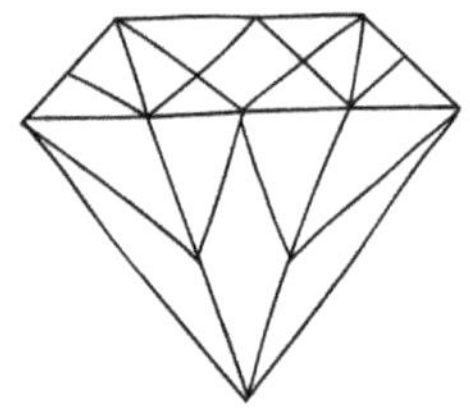

Mean girls are mean,
and there's no need for meanness.
It's their insecurity showing, but it takes
years to figure that out.

But bitches? They're great.
Bitches take no shit,
or they've reached their limit.
Bitches are made, not born.
We get shit done.
We insist upon boundaries.
Bitches COME.
(Yeah, sex exists for us, too.)

Mean girls, on the other hand, want to be
wanted.
Maybe bitches do, too,
But not at our own expense.

Bitches get divorced.
Mean girls run the PTA,
Policing the snacks, from the trunks of their
white SUVs,
mostly Range Rovers.
Bitter wine moms,
sipping from their coffee mugs.
Bitches rally.
Bitches protest.
They are fierce protectors
who raise angry girls.

Guilty Again

The woman who wants
is guilty again.
Guilty for wanting
for not always smiling
while wearing shoes that pinch her toes.

For not embodying your bro-pastor's
Mother's Day sermon on sacrifice,
full of dad jokes and sports metaphors.
He caters to men every service,
even on her day.

What woman wants is too much.
Food, but not too much!
(You might take up space.)
A drink, but not too much!
(You might get raped.)
Sex? (What's wrong with her, anyway?)
Clothes? (She's clearly filling a void in her
marriage.)
Her car? It must be for the children.
She gardens? They must not be having sex
at home.

When a woman wants,
She wants too much.
When men want,
we call it leadership.
Admired ambition.
It's in their nature.

The wanting woman?
She's guilty again.

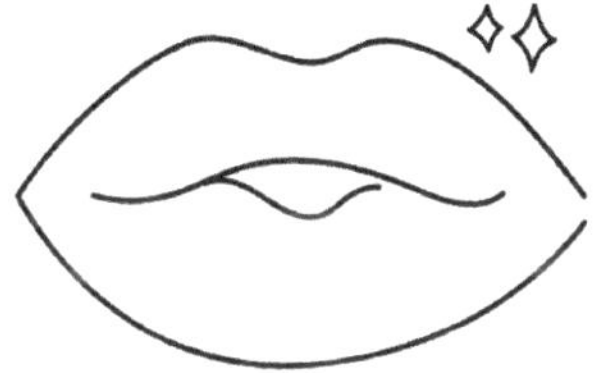

Italy

I'll take Italy over France any day.
Venice over Paris.
Food over their stiff fashions.
Fast cars over another blue cheese.

Sure, I know I'm romanticizing it.
When you visit, you can ignore politics and
savor moments—
Sex and wine and food and fashion and cars
and sun and water and lemon trees.
Beauty and splendor,
coast to coast.

"May I kiss your wife?," our driver for the
week asked, when dropping us at our last
stop, the airport.
He was an older gentleman,
and I was struck by the differences in the
two men before me.
One, my wealthy young husband, who
looked to me, knowing that was really a
question for me to answer, but so
disempowered by life he could not just

enjoy the moment and nod yes, as I did, to
the *gentiluomo*, who knew how to enjoy life.

What kind of man can't enjoy Italy?
It's no wonder we didn't stay married.

She Said

Another "he said/she said," they said.
She said he did, and
he said, "Not me."
He said, "Well, maybe I'll just say you did
the same to me."
"How about that?"
he said.

She said it again.
They said an awful lot of nothing,
with their prepared remarks,
coached by coaches,
their story straight(ened).

"But he's been to my house!"
other men say.
"Surely not!"
they claim in defense of their friend
"Why, he's met my wife."
"These boys would never…"

Despite what she said.
And she said.
And she said.

And she said.
"Me too," they said.
But he said "regretted sex,"
and they said, "Insufficient evidence."

Desperately Seeking

We grew up in the 80s.
The time of desperate ambition.
The time of Madonna, Michael Jackson,
George Michael, of MTV.

We saw them work for it.
They showed us.
We witnessed their fame come at a cost.
Wanting so bad they could taste it.
Us trying to taste them through the screen.
All of desperately seeking
Freedom
Artistic control
Trying to preserve their sanity
Giving us their own version of
behind-the-scenes footage.
We couldn't deny they worked hard,
Giving us what we wanted.
She asked, "What are you looking at?"
The heyday of music video.
My Roman empire.

Roses

Turns out, I'm good at growing roses
through almost total neglect of the plant.

I think we have an understanding, me and
the roses bushes.
We make sense to each other.
These are garden roses
not the long stems of bouquets.

These are hardy,
beautiful,
thorny.
They climb rock walls around our home.
They outlast the marriage.

I like that they refuse to die
even after I've left,
reminding my husband that the house is
really mine,
that I'm still there and will be,
no matter what he does with it.

In moments of anger, I consider taking the
roses bushes with me.

I imagine just pulling the plants from the
ground as I walk out.
I imagine transplanting them across town,
where I've landed.

But we agreed no, the roses would stay.
I thought he needed beauty,
whether he knew it or not.
Taking them would only make this sadder.

Each spring they bloom
And we all know I was there.

NYE

The glitter from my dress still lives in my
car, to this day.
That dress was a cheap one,
but looked good.

I promised you a midnight kiss.
Just for fun,
just to stave off loneliness
because you deserve to be kissed
and we have fun together,
and it *was* fun.

It started soft, with laughter,
and we took it from there.

We laughed (then and now),
cause we upset the bitchy wine moms
who think that club is theirs,
for we weren't playing by the rules.

We refuse to play the parts they play,
since they've traded sex for wealth.
We're supposed to drink and judge each
other,
Not take joy where we find it.
Especially outside the bounds of the hetero
compromise.

They can keep self-medicating in the
suffocation of their gated communities,
competing in the losing game that it is their
continual crisis of aging,
Trying to look good,
not for their average, drooping husbands,
maybe partly for themselves
but mostly in competition,
The pageant being the real housewives of
legal prostitution.
The "real" housewives with their fake teeth,
fake hair, fake tits, and fake orgasms.

Our real is hot,
Alive and considerate
Healthy
Expressive
Exploratory
Loving
Lustful.

We held hands on the way home,
feeling the very real warmth that comes with
the love of real women,
real friends.

Bubbles and the Oak Tree

This sounds like the title of a children's
book, but it is a tribute to the glue of our
friend group.

They organize and answer,
set up and take down,
love and laugh.
They show up.
They forgive,
extend grace,
listen and plan,
cook and decorate and keep our traditions
going.

I worry that they live underappreciated.
Please know that I am so thankful for you,
these friends few of us deserve.

Drunk Sweet

He's drunk again,
but he's a sweet drunk,
not angry, so it's okay.

He reeks of liquor and cigarette smoke, she
thinks to herself, as he climbs into bed.
He snuggles up against her.
He says he is so lucky
He says that he loves her
That he likes her
So much.

He's affectionate, not sexual, in these
moments.
So much like a lost boy come home to his
mother.

He'll want to fuck her in the morning,
when he sees her differently,
when he wakes with inexplicable energy.

But even as he says his profane thoughts she
loves to hear, he nestles his face in her
breasts.

He sighs and visibly relaxes with his face
there.
He feels safe for a moment.

Do they all want to fuck their mothers?
Not literally, of course,
but subconsciously?

Even her most experienced, lusty lovers still
cast her as both madonna and whore,
Believing they are conquering something as
they fuck her with their swords as
temperamental as Italian sports cars.

Men.
Sigh.
They're so tortured and trapped, performing
the false bravado of American masculinity,
Craving the very emasculation that drives
their ridiculous temper tantrums,
whether road rage or war.

At least this one is sweet and seeks pleasure
where can find it,
channeling his demons into naughty
consensual sex,
as dirty as she'll allow.

He's an artist and a dancer.
He knows how to move while inside her.
He can move his hips.
He can make her come.
He makes her breakfast, afterwards, in the
morning.

Hot Asphalt

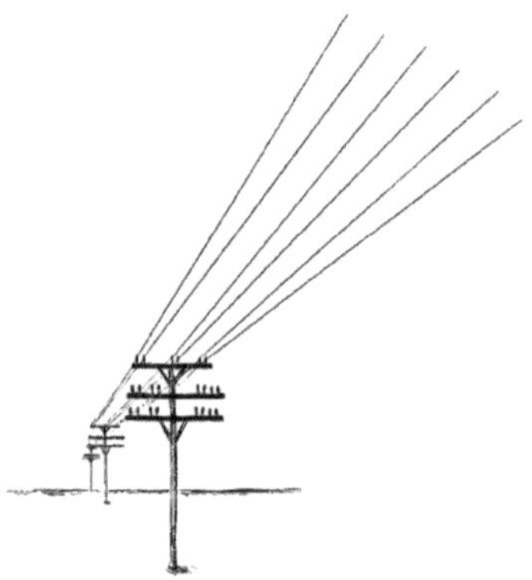

Does any moment hold more possibility than
a late morning in early summer,
the cheerful smell of suntan oil coming off
their warm bodies,
two of the many bodies who had come to
cool off in the crisp blue water.

Upbeat disposable pop music plays in the
background.
Girls browse magazines or read books,
in those years before the internet and cell
phones.

Boys would see them and brainstorm ways
to "accidentally" run into the girls, maybe in
line at the concession stand.

Girls would also look at them,
Some harboring secret crushes, but they
assumed they were straight.
It seemed like everyone was then.

Fathers would see the girls and fantasize as
if statutory rape weren't a crime.
Mothers liked the girls, who were so
well-behaved and pretty, and they would say
hi and send their regards to their mother,
then run a hand over their middle-aged
bodies and sigh.

The sunlight reflects off the water;
The heat, off the pale concrete of the deck,
while the parking lot asphalt absorbs the
sun's rays, giving off its hot smell by
midday.

Campers meant strangers, in a good way.
New people.

Locals from all three surrounding counties
would come to their small town during the
summer, just for the park,
and then, for a chance to see them.

They lived at the park that summer.
A regular feature.
"Turn around," one of the older lifeguards
said to the outgoing sister.
He elbowed his buddy.
"How old do you think she is?" he asked.
"Nineteen?" the friend guesses.
"Thirteen," he answers emphatically,
conveying disbelief.
They shake their heads and laugh, and then
motion her away.

Was that thrilling or gross?
Did that feel safe, or risky?
The not knowing how to feel is what
adolescence feels like, she thinks to herself
years later.
As a teen, you just exist between those two
states.

Back then, it seemed that meeting a new boy
could change her life on a dime.

Now, when they approach, she inwardly
groans and thinks, "Not again."

At forty, she welcomes a more direct
approach.
Even impersonal, when she can get it.
A truck driver who honks at her as she
drives her nice car, singing loudly as she
speeds on the interstate.

At forty, this is the better compliment,
the honk and the wave and a smile.
They expect nothing else from her.

No, thankfully, this won't change her life.
But for a moment it will brighten her day.

Company Policy

Why was it my job today
to make my white
cisgender
heterosexual
male
boss
feel better?

Because I had the audacity to tell him the
people had questions about our school
arresting protestors.

Ouch.
Wounded.
Surprised, even?

This man leaned his head against the wall,
sitting in silence for so long that I finally
asked, "What's going on over there?"
(buddy)
the way I would ask a second grader.

"Why don't people give us the benefit of the
doubt?" he asks.

It's a sincere question.

I'm still stunned, hours later.
(He's forty.)

There are no limits to the white man's faith
in institutions.
(My god.)

"History is the proof to the contrary,"
I gently break it to him.

I ruined his day.
He's never considered how the institutions
ruin lives, as people like him follow their
neatly written policies.

They will kill us all, I realize again.
Per company policy.
We dare to make them reflect upon it and
we're the problems, every one.

www.ingramcontent.com/pod-product-compliance
Lightning Source LLC
LaVergne TN
LVHW050310210726
843507LV00020B/2670